Unleash Your Online Potential

Learn How to Start a Profitable
Internet Business Today!

by
Phillip Sheffield

DISCLAIMER

CONTENT

CHAPTER 1

Introduction

This book is focused on helping readers to start and grow their own profitable online business. It is meant to empower readers with the knowledge, tools, and strategies they need to bring their online business ideas to life and succeed in the competitive world of e-commerce.

The book, "Unleash Your Online Potential," is meant to evoke a sense of untapped potential and opportunity. The phrase "online potential" suggests that there is a world of possibilities waiting to be explored on the internet, and the article aims to help readers unlock that potential.

Overall, the goal of this book is to inspire and empower readers to take control of their financial future by starting their own online business. Whether they are looking to generate a side income or build a full-time career, the article provides the tools and resources that are needed to get started and succeed in the fast-paced world of e-commerce.

CHAPTER 2

Start Point Of Online Money Making

The starting point of making money online is you, and not the methods, search engines, supposed "secrets", or so-called experts. If you adopt this mindset and follow these guidelines, you can achieve success in making money online, irrespective of any past unsuccessful attempts, previous failures, or current feelings of discouragement.

The key to success in any venture, including making money online, is to have a clear and focused goal and the determination to achieve it. It requires a great deal of effort, energy, and time to create a successful online business or source of income. Often, people fail to understand the level of commitment and persistence required to succeed in this field, and they give up too soon, even after a few weeks or months. Unlike a traditional job where you have a clear job description, set working hours, and a fixed salary, making money online is more fluid and requires an entrepreneurial mindset.

You must be willing to take risks, experiment with different approaches, and continuously learn and adapt to new trends and technologies. It is a process that takes time and dedication, and success does not come overnight.

Therefore, if you want to succeed in making money online, you need to have a long-term perspective and focus your energy on one goal or project at a time. Avoid the temptation to jump from one shiny object to another, as this will only lead to frustration and disappointment. Instead, set realistic goals, create a plan, and work tirelessly towards achieving them. With enough persistence, commitment, and hard work, you can create a successful online business and generate a sustainable income.

It is true that there are several ways to earn a decent income online. Whether it's creating videos, podcasting, selling information products, affiliate marketing, or consulting, there are various opportunities to monetize your skills and expertise. However, the common thread that runs through all successful online businesses is the focus on one specific area.

When you try to do too many things at once, you dilute your energy, focus, and efforts. It becomes difficult to achieve excellence in any one area, and success may remain elusive. Therefore, the key is to pick one specific area and concentrate your efforts on it for a full year. This is not to say that you cannot diversify or explore other opportunities in the future, but you must devote yourself to one area first.

When you focus on one area, you can channel all your energy, time, and resources towards it. You can become an expert in that field, gain credibility, and build a loyal following. The money will naturally follow if you provide value and solve problems for your audience or customers. The goal should not be to make money but to be the best at what you do.

Success in making money online is not a get-rich-quick scheme, but a long-term process that requires persistence, dedication, and hard work. It takes time to build a sustainable income stream, and you may experience setbacks and failures along the way. However, if you follow this approach and put in the necessary effort, you will eventually achieve success and financial freedom.

CHAPTER 3

Finding Your Motivation And Realizing Your Achievements Each Day.

The primary reason why people struggle to stay committed or concentrate on a task is often due to the lack of a powerful motivation for doing so. It is essential to recognize that having a strong reason why you are pursuing a particular goal is critical to your success. When you have a clear and powerful motivation for doing something, you are more likely to stick to it even when faced with obstacles, setbacks, or challenges.

Your motivation could be driven by a sense of purpose, a desire to make a positive impact, or a personal goal that is deeply meaningful to you. It is this motivation that keeps you going when things get tough, and it inspires you to push through adversity. On the other hand, if you lack a compelling reason for pursuing a particular goal, you are more likely to give up when faced with obstacles.

Without a clear motivation, it is easy to become distracted, lose focus, or get discouraged when things do not go as planned.

Therefore, it is crucial to identify your reason for pursuing any goal or endeavor. This motivation will provide you with the energy and drive to keep going, even when the going gets tough. When you have a powerful reason why, you are more likely to see things through to the end and achieve the success you desire. it's important to realize that starting a business or any new endeavor is rarely easy. It takes hard work, dedication, and persistence to achieve success. Therefore, it's essential to have a powerful reason for wanting to start a business or earn more income.

Your motivation could be driven by a desire to achieve financial freedom, provide for your family, pursue your passion, or make a positive impact in the world. Whatever your reason why, it needs to be strong enough to keep you motivated when the going gets tough. The early stages of any business venture are typically the most challenging, and it's during this time that many people give up. However, if you have a powerful motivation for starting your business, you will be more likely to push through the challenges and keep working towards your goal.

Having a strong reason why also helps you to stay focused and avoid distractions. When you have a clear motivation, it's easier to prioritize your time and energy and avoid getting sidetracked by things that are not aligned with your goals.

In summary, having a strong reason why is critical to your success in any endeavor, including starting a business or earning more income. It provides you with the motivation and focus to push through the challenges and achieve your goals. What is your motivation for desiring financial success? Is it the pursuit of freedom, wealth, time, revenge, love, or family? It is crucial to ensure that your motivation is powerful and significant enough to withstand the inevitable periods of doubt, fear, and disappointment.

CHAPTER 4

Guidelines For Achieving Success In An Internet Marketing Career.

The adage "You need money to make money"

It is best if you have a source of income already. While making money online can be a lucrative venture, it is important to keep in mind that it takes time and effort to build a successful online business. Thus, having a stable source of income, such as a job, can provide you with the financial security you need to invest in your online ventures and also cover your basic living expenses.

Many people make the mistake of quitting their jobs prematurely in pursuit of making money online. However, this can lead to financial difficulties and stress, as they do not have a stable income to rely on. It is advisable to keep your job while you build your online business, especially in the initial stages. If you do not have a job and are struggling financially, it is recommended that you focus on finding a steady source of income first.

Trying to make money online when you have no money to invest can be challenging, and it may take longer to see any significant results. Thus, it is advisable to get a job with a steady paycheck and use your free time to build your online business. By doing this, you will have the financial security you need to invest in your online ventures without the added stress of bills piling up.

You Can't Spread Yourself Too Thin

It's essential to focus on one thing at a time when it comes to making money online. Trying to do too many things at once can lead to burnout and decreased effectiveness. Many people fall into the trap of attempting to start multiple online businesses or pursuing various marketing strategies simultaneously, but this approach rarely leads to success. Instead, choose one business or marketing strategy and devote all your attention and effort to it until it succeeds or you realize it's not viable. Once you have established one source of income, you can expand and diversify. While having enthusiasm and a desire to explore various areas is admirable, it may not be feasible. Trying to do too many things at once can result in failure.

Immediate Outcomes Cannot Be Anticipated.

Getting acquainted with the top online marketers will reveal that they've experienced more failures than successes. It took some of them months to start generating income, but they understood that continuous learning and progress were crucial for eventual success. Without a safety net, stress can lead to panic and poor decision-making. However, with a job that covers your bills, you can acquire knowledge and implement it at a comfortable pace. This financial security eliminates the need for immediate results, enabling you to figure things out gradually and arrive at a viable solution.

Don't Give Up Easily

Some individuals expect instant gratification and give up too easily on Internet Marketing because they think it should be easy. The passage implies that if success in Internet Marketing was a straightforward and effortless endeavor, then everyone would be doing it and enjoying the benefits of working from home or exotic locations with hired help.

However, the reality is that Internet Marketing is a complex field that requires dedication, effort, and a willingness to learn and adapt to new technologies and trends. Those who expect instant results and quit before they fully comprehend the process are unlikely to succeed in this field. Success in Internet Marketing is achievable but requires time, effort, and perseverance.

Similar to how a professional athlete undergoes continuous training, if your objective is to generate income online, you need to engage in uninterrupted reading, studying, implementing, and testing. If you have a strong desire to succeed, you must be willing to focus on the work and put in the effort. Approach this endeavor with the understanding that you will persevere and never give up. If you make a commitment to yourself to keep going, you will eventually find a way to succeed. By promising yourself that you will never give up and having the persistence to keep going, you will eventually find a way to achieve success. The passage highlights that the key to success in online ventures is dedication, perseverance, and a willingness to put in the necessary work to achieve your goals.

A Better Approach Is To Diversify

After selecting an opportunity to pursue in the field of internet marketing, it is essential to diversify as much as possible. This is because internet marketing is a dynamic industry that is constantly evolving due to changes in technology, consumer behavior, and market trends. Diversification is the process of spreading one's resources and investments across multiple options to reduce the overall risk of failure. In internet marketing, diversification could mean exploring different niches, using different platforms and channels to reach audiences, and leveraging multiple revenue streams.

For instance, an internet marketer who focuses solely on one product or service risks losing everything if that single offering becomes outdated or less popular. However, if they diversify their offerings and explore various niches, they have a higher chance of success, as they have multiple sources of income and can pivot their focus if one area becomes less profitable. Diversification is essential in internet marketing because the industry is continually evolving. By spreading resources across multiple opportunities, marketers can reduce the risk of failure and increase their chances of success.

Starting Out, It's Essential To Embrace Minimalism.

It's important not to be like those who, upon earning their first significant amount of money, rush to spend it on frivolous material possessions like an expensive watch, as this can lead to failure. Instead, it's essential to stay grounded and maintain focus. Losing focus can lead to failure quickly.

When starting out in any business or venture, it is crucial to maintain focus and discipline. The pursuit of material possessions can be a distraction from the essential goals and objectives of the venture. In internet marketing, for instance, early success can be exciting and lead to a sense of invincibility, which can then lead to reckless spending and poor decision-making. By remaining grounded and focused on the goals of the venture, one can avoid such pitfalls. Losing focus can cause a rapid decline in performance, leading to failure. It is, therefore, vital to stay disciplined and focus on building a solid foundation that can withstand the inevitable challenges and setbacks that come with any venture.

It's important not to aim to impress others since it won't increase your earnings.

It's recommended to spend your money on essential items that can improve your online business, such as a high-speed computer, modern smartphone, online tools and software, advertising, and cameras (if you create video content). At the same time, it's important to evaluate your expenses and seek ways to reduce unnecessary spending. A high-speed computer or laptop is an essential item for any online entrepreneur as it enables them to work more efficiently and effectively. A modern smartphone is also crucial as it allows business owners to stay connected and engaged with their customers on the go. Online tools and software, such as project management and accounting software, can help automate and streamline business operations, saving time and effort. Investing in advertising can also be beneficial, as it can help to drive traffic and increase brand awareness. Creating video content is another effective way to engage customers, and cameras are necessary tools for this. It's essential to prioritize expenses that can have a direct impact on the success of the business while avoiding frivolous spending that won't contribute to business growth.

It's Crucial To Save Money.

The above point is relevant here too. It's important not to spend all your money when you start making a profit. Instead, set aside some funds for future needs. As a self-employed individual, it's crucial to think about the big picture since there are no health benefits, retirement funds, or other perks that come with being an employee. You are solely responsible for your future.

If you start making money online, it's advisable to hire an accountant to manage your finances and work with a financial adviser to plan your savings and investments. This will help you secure your financial future, so you won't regret spending all your money on frivolous things in your old age.

It's essential to have fun and enjoy your success, but it's equally important not to overspend.

Instead, focus on saving money and spending wisely. By prioritizing saving over spending, you can ensure long-term financial stability and security.

Internet Marketing Should Be Treated As A Legitimate Business.

Many individuals make the mistake of thinking that they can work whenever they want and still succeed in internet marketing due to the lifestyle that is portrayed. However, this is far from the truth. Internet marketing should be treated like a legitimate business, and hard work is required for success. If you were working at a regular job, you would be terminated instantly if you showed up or left as you pleased. Therefore, approach your online business with the same level of dedication as you would with a traditional job. Even though internet marketing offers the advantage of working from anywhere in the world and having flexible hours, it is crucial to establish a set schedule for work and uphold it.

To be successful in internet marketing, it's important to maintain a professional image and approach to your business dealings. This means being prompt and responsive when it comes to emails and addressing any issues that may arise in a timely manner. Remember that internet marketing is a real business, and treating it as such will help you establish a strong reputation and build trust with your customers or clients.

CHAPTER 5

Opportunities

Selling Services

Selling services involves offering your knowledge, abilities, or aid to customers or clients and receiving payment in return. It encompasses various fields, such as freelance writing, graphic design, web development, consulting, or coaching. The process of selling services includes recognizing a market need, promoting one's proficiency, determining the appropriate rates, and delivering satisfactory results or assistance to clients. It may also necessitate building a reputable brand, establishing connections with potential customers, and gaining trust and reliability in the respective field.

Offering basic services such as graphic design, research, ghostwriting, finder's assistance, programming, and more to other businesses or individuals. It's important to recognize that competition in the field of selling services can be intense.

In most cases, many individuals are offering similar services, leading to oversupply and reduced demand. As a result, buyers may not be willing to pay high prices due to the abundance of options available unless you excel exceptionally in the specific skill they require.

Success in this business depends on having specialized skills, experience, and patience. However, the amount of money you can make is limited by several factors, including the number of hours you can work each day, the number of clients you can serve in that time, the volume of job offers you receive, the level of competition offering the same services as you, and how much less you're willing to charge to avoid losing a client to a cheaper competitor. To succeed, you need to be patient, build your network, consistently deliver high-quality work, retain your clients, and continue to grow your business over time.

Selling Physical Products

To sell physical products means to offer tangible goods to customers in exchange for payment. This can involve a diverse range of products and industries, from clothing and accessories to household items, electronics, and beyond. Typically, selling physical products entails identifying a market need or a niche, sourcing or manufacturing products, setting suitable prices, and delivering high-quality products to customers. Additionally, building a strong brand, promoting products through various channels, and providing excellent customer service can help in retaining customers and driving repeat purchases.

Your personal flair, which translates to how much you prioritize your customers and strive to provide them with the best products, is essential to the success of any business you venture into, including this one. The current trend in advertising is focused on internet-based business models such as mini-importation and e-commerce.

To get started properly, Initially, it is essential to acquire the appropriate type of authentic goods. Furthermore, you will have to contend with Customs regulations, which can impact your profits. Additionally, marketing your goods will require investment, both monetarily and through physical effort. Establishing a brand is also crucial as it instills trust in potential customers.

The physical product import and resale business has the potential to be extremely lucrative, provided that you are knowledgeable about the precise procedures and confidential strategies required to generate substantial profits. Nevertheless, acquiring such valuable information is unlikely to be offered for free. Often, obtaining such detailed strategies requires payment, and the fees can sometimes be substantial. Essential Skills: Web Design, Offer

Development, Formulating a Marketing Plan, Autoresponder Integration, Generating Traffic, Managing Inventory, Providing Customer Support, Implementing Upselling Techniques, and more.

Information Publishing

If you have a passion for teaching, possess excellent writing skills, and have access to valuable knowledge that others are willing to pay a substantial amount for, then the information marketing industry may be an excellent fit for you.

As an information marketer, you do not necessarily have to be the foremost authority on the subject matter of the information you sell. You can always collaborate with someone who possesses expertise in the relevant field. However, to succeed in this field, you must offer valuable information that people are willing to pay for. There are numerous information categories where individuals are willing to invest significant sums, and these are the markets you should target. If you aim to generate substantial revenue as an information marketer, you must offer more than just eBooks. You should provide home

study courses, live seminars, coaching programs, and more.
Essential Skills: Technical Aptitude, Marketing Expertise, Traffic Generation Strategies, Inventory Management, Customer Support, and more.

Consultancy/Coaching

Consulting or coaching involves selling your time and expertise to provide advice to clients. It is similar to information marketing, with the distinction being that you are not offering a set of materials for clients to study. Instead, you provide clients with access to your knowledge and experience in a specific subject area. Additionally, in some cases, you may even assist clients in implementing the advice you provide. Essential Skills: Highly Specialized Knowledge and Expertise in a Particular Subject Area.

Affiliate Marketing

Affiliate marketing involves promoting and selling products or services belonging to other individuals or companies, in exchange for a commission on the sales made through your affiliate link or referral code.

In affiliate marketing, your role is to direct traffic and potential customers to the products or services of other businesses, thus saving them the expenses of advertising and promotion. In return, you receive a commission for every successful lead or sale made through your referral link or code. The range of products and services available for affiliate marketing is vast, including digital and physical products, offline services, software, and personalized solutions, among others. You can join various affiliate programs through different networks such as Clickbank.com and Verve Direct, Lemon Ads, A4D, Commission Junction (CJ) among others. You can either directly approach a company or register for an affiliate program through a network.

To succeed in affiliate marketing, it is crucial to select a company with a product or service that has a high sales record. This indicates that they have already identified their target market and optimized their offer, making it easier for your marketing efforts to drive traffic and generate sales. Required skills: marketing, traffic generation.

Creating Video Content.

Video content creation involves producing videos and uploading them to your YouTube channel, then monetizing the content in various ways such as enabling Google AdSense. This allows Google to run ads on your videos and pay you a percentage of the revenue collected from the advertisers. Alternatively, you can sell your own published information to your channel's subscribers and viewers, or promote other people's products and services as an affiliate and earn a commission on sales generated by your channel. Another option is to offer sponsored placements inside your videos, where companies pay you to showcase their products or services. This opportunity typically arises when your channel gains significant popularity. It requires a considerable amount of patience as it takes time to gain momentum.

Conclusively, It is important to select a business model that aligns with your personality, skills, and strengths. The reason being that it has been observed that the second most common cause of failure is attempting business models that do not fit their skill set. The issue with this is that it can take a considerable amount of time, perhaps years, to develop the necessary skills to succeed. Opting for a business model that matches your skills or can be quickly acquired leads to faster success and achieving your goals.

Selecting and operating within a business model that aligns with your skillset or can be rapidly acquired enables you to attain success and achieve your objectives more swiftly.